90

KEEPSAKES

SPRING

First published in the United States by
Salem House Publishers, 1989, 462 Boston Street,
Topsfield, Massachusetts, 01983.

Copyright © Swallow Publishing Ltd 1989

Conceived and produced by
Swallow Books, 260 Pentonville Road,
London N1 9JY

ISBN: 0 88162 379 2
Art Director: Elaine Partington
Editor: Catherine Tilley
Designer: Jean Hoyes
Picture Researcher: Liz Eddison
Printed in Hong Kong by Imago Publishing Limited

KEEPSAKES

SPRING

Compiled by
Audrey Williams

Salem House

The Thaw Comes

Frost-locked all the winter,
    Seeds, and roots, and stones of fruits,
What shall make their sap ascend
    That they may put forth shoots?
Tips of tender green,
    Leaf, or blade, or sheath;
Telling of the hidden life
    That breaks forth underneath,
Life nursed in its grave by Death.

Blows the thaw-wind pleasantly,
    Drips the soaking rain,
By fits looks down the waking sun:
    Young grass springs on the plain,
Young leaves clothe early hedgerow trees;
    Seeds, and roots, and stones of fruits,
Swollen with sap put forth their shoots;
    Curled-headed ferns sprout in the lane,
Birds sing and pair again.

CHRISTINA GEORGINA ROSSETTI

Elusive Changes

HERE ARE suggestions that Spring is a let-down; it does not come as it should, with a sudden glory. People who have known the season in other countries are unable to forget its contrasts with what has gone before. In place of a shout (they say), we have only a whisper: the green comes stealthily, if it has ever been absent; the season limps and hesitates, and brings nothing to sing about. Yet the birds seem not to agree. As dawn comes earlier, new voices are heard from the garden, and the trees are in a shrill commotion....

Spring can be hard to find: perhaps it comes to people at different times and in different ways. Some can wake on a particular morning and know that the change is here. The day need not be perfect; it may even be a little wild – the trees bending, and the sky clouded and moving; and yet in spite of the cloud there is no greyness, and the air can be tasted.... Doubters may wait, until in the end not even they can fail to note the prodigious growth of weeds. Most infallible sign, however, is the appearance of small boys with kites. Nobody tells them the time has come: they simply know; and the message is heard by every generation. Birds and children understand these things better than we do.

M. H. HOLCROFT

New Suits

Now Time throws off his cloak again
   Of ermined frost, and wind, and rain,
And clothes him in the embroidery
   Of glittering sun and clear blue sky.
With beast and bird the forest rings,
   Each in his jargon cries or sings;
And Time throws off his cloak again
   Of ermined frost, and wind, and rain.

River, and fount, and tinkling brook
   Wear in their dainty livery
Drops of silver jewelry;
   In new-made suit they merry look;
And Time throws off his cloak again
   Of ermined frost, and wind, and rain.

CHARLES D'ORLEANS
translated by Henry Wadsworth Longfellow

Thy smiles I note, sweet early flower,
   That peeping from thy rustic bower
The festive news to earth dost bring,
   A fragrant messenger of Spring.

SAMUEL TAYLOR COLERIDGE

Jewel of Time

IT IS NOW spring, a time blessed by the heavens for the comfort of the world. Now the sun begins to give light to the air, and with the reflection of its beams to warm the cold earth. The beasts of the woods look out onto the plains, and fish from the deep run up into shallow waters. Breeding fowls start building their nests, and senseless creatures gather life into their bodies. Birds tune their throats to entertain the rising sun, and little flies begin to flock in the air. Now Cupid begins to gather his arrows and sharpen their heads. Time is now gracious in nature, and nature in time. The air is wholesome and the earth pleasant, and the sea is not uncomfortable. The aged feel a kind of youthfulness, and youth the spirit of life. Spring is the messenger of many pleasures: the courtiers' progress and the farmers' profit, the labourers' harvest and the beggars' pilgrimage. In short, there is much good to be spoken of at this season of the year. It is the jewel of time and the joy of nature.

NICHOLAS BRETON

A Spring Morning

The Spring comes in with all her hues and smells,
    In freshness breathing over hills and dells;
O'er woods where May her gorgeous drapery flings,
    And meads washed fragrant by their laughing springs.
Fresh are new opened flowers, untouched and free
    From the bold rifling of the amorous bee.
The happy time of singing birds is come,
    And Love's lone pilgrimage now finds a home;
Among the mossy oaks now coos the dove,
    And the hoarse crow finds softer notes for love.
The foxes play around their dens, and bark
    In joy's excess, 'mid woodland shadows dark.
The flowers join lips below; the leaves above;
    And every sound that meets the ear is Love.

JOHN CLARE

Hear how the birds, on ev'ry bloomy spray,
    With joyous musick wake the dawning day!
Why sit we mute when early linnets sing,
    When warbling Philomel salutes the spring?

ALEXANDER POPE

April Gossip

HE OLD WOMAN tried to let the cuckoo out of the basket at Heathfield fair as usual on the 14th; but there seems to have been a hitch with the lid, for he was not heard immediately about the country. Just before that two little boys were getting over a gate from a hop-garden, with handfuls of Lent lilies – a beautiful colour under the dark sky. They grow wild round the margin of the hop-garden, showing against the bare dark loam; gloomy cloud over and gloomy earth under. 'Sell me a bunch?' 'No, no, can't do that; we wants these yer for granmer.' 'Well, get me a bunch presently, and I will give you twopence for it.' 'I dunno. We sends the bunches we finds up to Aunt Polly in Lunnon, and they sends us back sixpence for every bunch.' So the wild flowers go to Lunnon from all parts of the country, bushels and bushels of them. Nearly two hundred miles away in Somerset a friend writes that he has been obliged to put up notice-boards to stay the people from tearing up his violets and primroses, not only gathering them but making the flowery banks waste; and notice-boards have proved no safeguard. The worst is that the roots are taken, so that years will be required to repair the loss.

RICHARD JEFFERIES

Cuckoo, Cuckoo

When daisies pied and violets blue
    And lady-smocks all silver white
And cuckoo-buds of yellow hue
    Do paint the meadows with delight,
The cuckoo then, on every tree,
    Mocks married men; for thus sings he, Cuckoo;
Cuckoo, cuckoo; O, word of fear,
    Unpleasing to a married ear!

When shepherds pipe on oaten straws,
    And merry larks are ploughmen's clocks,
When turtles tread, and rooks, and daws,
    And maidens bleach their summer smocks,
The cuckoo then, on every tree,
    Mocks married men; for thus sings he, Cuckoo;
Cuckoo, cuckoo; O, word of fear,
    Unpleasing to a married ear!

WILLIAM SHAKESPEARE

May Day

A s I WAS lying in bed this morning, enjoying one of those half-dreams, half-reveries, which are so pleasant in the country, when the birds are singing about the window, and the sunbeams peeping through the curtains, I was roused by the sound of music. On going down-stairs, I found a number of villagers dressed in their holiday clothes, bearing a pole ornamented with garlands and ribands, and accompanied by the village band of music, under the direction of the tailor, the pale fellow who plays on the clarionet. They had all sprigs of hawthorn, or, as it is called 'the May,' in their hats, and had brought green branches and flowers to decorate the Hall door and windows. They have come to give notice that the May-pole was reared on the green and to invite the household to witness the sports.... Before reaching the village, I saw the May-pole towering above the cottages, with its gay garlands and streamers, and heard the sound of music. I found that there had been booths set up near it, for the reception of company; and a bower of green branches and flowers for the Queen of May, a fresh, rosy-cheeked girl of the village.

WASHINGTON IRVING

Spring

Nothing is so beautiful as Spring—
    When weeds, in wheels, shoot long and lovely and lush;
Thrush's eggs look little low heavens, and thrush
    Through the echoing timber does so rinse and wring
The ear, it strikes like lightnings to hear him sing;
    'The glassy peartree leaves and blooms, they brush
The descending blue; that blue is all in a rush
    With richness; the racing lambs too have fair their fling.

What is all this juice and all this joy?
    A strain of the earth's sweet being in the beginning
In Eden garden. – Have, get, before it cloy,

Before it cloud, Christ, lord, and sour with sinning,
    Innocent mind and Mayday in girl and boy,
Most, O maid's child, thy choice and worthy the winning.

GERARD MANLEY HOPKINS

A Lakeside Walk

THURSDAY 15TH APRIL 1802. It was a threatening misty morning – but mild. We set off after dinner from Eusemere. When we were in the woods beyond Gowbarrow park we saw a few daffodils close to the water side. We fancied that the lake had floated the seeds ashore and that the little colony had so sprung up. But as we went along there were more and yet more and at last under the boughs of the trees, we saw that there was a long belt of them along the shore, about the breadth of a country turnpike road. I never saw daffodils so beautiful they grew among the mossy stones about and about them, some rested their heads upon these stones as on a pillow for weariness and the rest tossed and reeled and danced and seemed as if they verily laughed with the wind that blew upon them over the lake, they looked so gay ever glancing ever changing. . . . The Bays were stormy, and we heard the waves at different distances and in the middle of the water like the sea. Rain came on – we were wet when we reached Luffs but we called in. Luckily all was chearless and gloomy so we faced the storm – we *must* have been wet if we had waited – put on dry clothes at Dobson's. I was very kindly treated by a young woman, the Landlady looked sour but it is her way. She gave us a goodish supper. Excellent ham and potatoes.

DOROTHY WORDSWORTH

The Sweet Spring!

Spring, the sweet Spring, is the year's pleasant king;
 Then blooms each thing, then maids dance in a ring,
Cold doth not sting, the pretty birds do sing,
 Cuckoo, jug-jug, pu-we, to-witta-woo!

The palm and may make country houses gay,
 Lambs frisk and play, the shepherds pipe all day,
And we hear aye birds tune this merry lay,
 Cuckoo, jug-jug, pu-we, to-witta-woo.

The fields breathe sweet, the daisies kiss our feet,
Young lovers meet, old wives a-sunning sit,
In every street these tunes our ears do greet,
 Cuckoo, jug-jug, pu-we, to-witta-woo!
  Spring! the sweet Spring!

THOMAS NASH

It was a lover and his lass,
 With a hey, and a ho, and a hey nonino,
That o'er the green corn-field did pass
 In the spring time, the only pretty ring time,
When birds do sing, hey ding a ding, ding:
 Sweet lovers love the spring.

WILLIAM SHAKESPEARE

Colonial Ways

N OUR ARRIVAL here the stalks of last year's crop still remained on the ground. At this I was greatly surprised, as the season was now so far advanced, I expected to have found the fields completely ploughed at least, if not sown and harrowed; but how much was my amazement increased to find that every instrument of husbandry was unknown here; not only all the various ploughs, but all the machinery used with such success at home, and that the only instrument used is a hoe, with which they at once till and plant the corn.... Here the wheel-plough would answer finely, as the ground is quite flat, the soil light and not a stone to be met with in a thousand acres. A drill too might easily be constructed for sowing the seed, and a light harrow would close it in with surprising expedition. It is easy to observe however from whence this ridiculous method of theirs took its first necessary rise. When the new Settlers were obliged to sow corn for their immediate maintenance, before they were able to root out the trees, it is plain no other instrument but the hoe could be used amongst the roots of the trees, where it was to be planted, and they were obliged to do it all by hand labour.

JANET SCHAW

Spring Flowers

Along the blushing borders, bright with dew,
    And in yon mingled wilderness of flowers,
Fair-handed Spring unbosoms every grace:
    Throws out the snow-drop, and the crocus first;
The daisy, primrose, violet darkly blue,
    And polyanthus of unnumber'd dyes;
The yellow wall-flower, stain'd with iron-brown;
    The lavish stock that scents the garden round:
From the soft wing of vernal breezes shed,
    Anemonies; auriculas, enrich'd
With shining meal o'er all their velvet leaves;
    And full renunculas, of glowing red.
Then comes the tulip-race, where beauty plays
    Her idle freaks: from family diffus'd
To family, as flies the father-dust,
    The varied colours run; and while they break
On the charm'd eye, th' exulting florist marks,
    With secret pride, the wonders of his hand.

JAMES THOMSON

Health in the Air

PRING DREW ON — she was indeed already come; the frosts of winter had ceased; its snows were melted, its cutting winds ameliorated. My wretched feet, flayed and swollen to lameness by the sharp air of January, began to heal and subside under the gentler breathings of April; the nights and mornings no longer by their Canadian temperature froze the very blood in our veins; we could now endure the play-hour passed in the garden; sometimes on a sunny day it began even to be pleasant and genial, and a greenness grew over those brown beds, which, freshening daily, suggested the thought that Hope traversed them at night, and left each morning brighter traces of her steps.... Flowers peeped out amongst the leaves: snowdrops, crocuses, purple auriculas, and golden-eyed pansies.

April advanced to May: a bright serene May it was; days of blue sky, placid sunshine, and soft western or southern gales filled up its duration. And now vegetation matured with vigour; Lowood shook loose its tresses; it became all green, all flowery; its great elm, ash, and oak skeletons were restored to majestic life; woodland plants sprang up profusely in its recesses; unnumbered varieties of moss filled its hollows, and it made a strange ground-sunshine out of the wealth of its wild primrose plants.

CHARLOTTE BRONTE

The Shepherd-Boys

The valley rings with mirth and joy;
    Among the hills the echoes play
A never never ending song,
    To welcome in the May.
The magpie chatters with delight;
    The mountain raven's youngling brood
Have left the mother and the nest;
    And they go rambling east and west
In search of their own food;
    Or through the glittering vapours dart
In very wantonness of heart.

Beneath a rock, upon the grass,
    Two boys are sitting in the sun;
Their work, if any work they have,
    Is out of mind – or done.
On pipes of sycamore they play
    The fragments of a Christmas hymn;
Or with that plant which in our dale
    We call stag-horn, or fox's tail,
Their rusty hats they trim:
    And thus, as happy as the day,
Those Shepherds wear the time away.

WILLIAM WORDSWORTH

Weather Forecasting

HE weather is a thing that is beyond me altogether. I never can understand it. The barometer is useless: it is as misleading as the newspaper forecast. There was one hanging up in a hotel at Oxford at which I was staying last spring, and, when I got there, it was pointing to 'set fair.' It was simply pouring with rain outside, and had been all day; and I couldn't quite make matters out. I tapped the barometer, and it jumped up and pointed to 'very dry.'.... I tapped it again the next morning, and it went up still higher, and the rain came down faster than ever. On Wednesday I went and hit it again, and the pointer went round towards 'set fair,' 'very dry,' and 'much heat,' until it was stopped by the peg, and couldn't go any further. It tried its best, but the instrument was built so that it couldn't prophesy fine weather any harder than it did without breaking itself. It evidently wanted to go on, and prognosticate drought, and water famine, and sunstroke, and simooms, and such things, but the peg prevented it, and it had to be content with pointing to the mere commonplace 'very dry.' Meanwhile, the rain came down in a steady torrent and the lower part of the town was under water, owing to the river having overflowed.

JEROME K. JEROME

To Spring

O thou with dewy locks, who lookest down
    Thro' the clear windows of the morning, turn
Thine angel eyes upon our western isle,
    Which in full choir hails thy approach, O Spring!

The hills tell each other, and the list'ning
    Vallies hear; all our longing eyes are turned
Up to thy bright pavillions: issue forth,
    And let thy holy feet visit our clime.

Come o'er the eastern hills, and let our winds
    Kiss thy perfumèd garments; let us taste
Thy morn and evening breath; scatter thy pearls
    Upon our love-sick land that mourns for thee.

O deck her forth with thy fair fingers; pour
    Thy soft kisses on her bosom; and put
Thy golden crown upon her languish'd head,
    Whose modest tresses were bound up for thee!

WILLIAM BLAKE

Queen o' the May

You must wake and call me early, call me early, mother dear,
   Tomorrow'll be the happiest time of all the glad New Year;
Of all the glad New Year, mother, the maddest, merriest day,
   For I'm to be Queen o' the May, mother, I'm to be Queen
     o' the May.

The honeysuckle round the porch has wov'n its wavy bowers,
   And by the meadow-trenches blow the faint, sweet cuckoo
     flowers,
And the wild marsh-marigold shines like fire in swamps and
     hollows grey,
   And I'm to be Queen o' the May, mother, I'm to be Queen
     o' the May.

All the valley, mother, will be fresh and green and still,
   And the cowslip and the crowfoot are over all the hill.
And the rivulet in the flowery dale'll merrily glance and play,
   For I'm to be Queen o' the May, mother, I'm to be Queen
     o' the May.

LORD TENNYSON

Hang Spring-Cleaning!

 HE MOLE had been working very hard all the morning, spring-cleaning his little home. First with brooms, then with dusters; then on ladders and steps and chairs, with a brush and a pail of whitewash; till he had dust in his throat and eyes, and splashes of whitewash all over his black fur, and an aching back and weary arms. Spring was moving in the air above and in the earth below and around him, penetrating even his dark and lowly little house with its spirit of divine discontent and longing. It was small wonder, then, that he suddenly flung down his brush on the floor, said 'Bother!' and 'O blow!' and also 'Hang spring-cleaning!' and bolted out of the house without even waiting to put on his coat. Something up above was calling him imperiously, and he made for the steep little tunnel which answered in his case to the gravelled carriage-drive owned by animals whose residences are near to the sun and air. So he scraped and scratched and scrabbled and scrooged, and then he scrooged again and scrabbled and scratched and scraped, working busily with his little paws and muttering to himself, 'Up we go! Up we go!' till at last, pop! his snout came out into the sunlight, and he found himself rolling in the warm grass of a great meadow.

KENNETH GRAHAME

A Time for Pilgrimage

When that April with his showers sweet
    The drought of March has pierced to the root,
And bathed every vein in sweet liquor
    Of which virtue engendered is the flower;
When Zephyrus also with his sweet breath
    Inspired has in every holt and heath
The tender crops, and the young sun
    Has in the Ram his half course run,
And small fowls make melody,
    That sleep all the night with open eye
(So prick them nature in their courage);
    Then folk long to go on pilgrimages,
And palmers for to seek strange shores,
    To remote parts, couched in sundry lands;
And specially from every shire's end
    Of England to Canterbury they wend,
The holy blissful martyr for to seek,
    That them has helped when that they were sick.

GEOFFREY CHAUCER

Sources and Acknowledgments

For permission to reproduce illustrations, the publishers thank the following: Bridgeman Art Library, Barbara Edwards, Sam Elder, Mary Evans Picture Library and E. T. Archive.

The extract from *The Journals of Dorothy Wordsworth* is reprinted by permission of Oxford University Press.